Identity Cause

Identity Cause

DAVID JAFFIN

First published in the United Kingdom in 2018 by
Shearsman Books
50 Westons Hill Drive
Emersons Green
Bristol BS16 7DF

Shearsman Books Ltd Registered Office
30–31 St. James Place, Mangotsfield, Bristol BS16 9JB
(this address not for correspondence)

www.shearsman.com

ISBN 978-1-84861-557-1

Distributed for Shearsman Books in the U. S. A.
by Small Press Distribution, 1341 Seventh Avenue, Berkeley, CA 94710
E-Mail orders@spdbooks.org
www.spdbooks.org

Production, composition, & cover design: Edition Wortschatz, a service of
Neufeld Verlag, Cuxhaven/Germany
E-Mail info@edition-wortschatz.de, www.edition-wortschatz.de

Title photograph:
Hannelore Bäumler, München

Printed in Germany

Contents

10

13

14

16

With continuing thanks
to Marina Moisel
for the preparation
of this manuscript

and to Hanni Bäumler
for her well-placed photograph

If I had to classify my poetry, it could best be done through the classical known "saying the most by using the least". The aim is thereby set: transparency, clarity, word-purity. Every word must carry its weight in the line and the ultimate aim is a unity of sound, sense, image and idea. Poetry, more than any other art, should seek for a unity of the senses, as the French Symbolists, the first poetic modernists, realized through the interchangeability of the senses: "I could hear the colors of her dress." One doesn't hear colors, but nevertheless there is a sensual truth in such an expression.

Essential is "saying the most by using the least". Compression is of the essence. And here are some of my most personal means of doing so turning verbs into nouns and the reverse, even within a double-context "Why do the leaves her so ungenerously behind". Breaking words into two or even three parts to enable both compression and the continuing flow of meaning. Those words must be placed back together again, thereby revealing their inner structure-atomising.

One of my critics rightly said: "Jaffin's poetry is everywhere from one seemingly unrelated poem to the next." Why? Firstly because of my education and interests trained at New York University as a cultural and intellectual historian. My doctoral dissertation on historiography emphasizes the necessary historical continuity. Today we often judge the past with the mind and mood of the present, totally contrary to their own historical context. I don't deny the past-romanticism and classical but integrate them within a singular modern context of word-usage and sensibility. Musically that would place me within the "classical-romantic tradition" of Haydn, Mozart, Mendelssohn, Brahms and Nielsen but at the very modern end of that tradition.

My life historically is certainly exceptional. My father was a prominent New York Jewish lawyer. The law never interested me, but history always did. A career as a cultural-intellectual historian was mine-for-the-asking, but I rejected historical relativism. That led me to a marriage with a devout German lady – so I took to a calling of Jesus-the-Jew in post-Auschwitz Germany. For ca. two decades I wrote and lectured all over Germany on Jesus the Jew. Thereby my knowledge and understanding of both interlocked religions became an essential part of my being. History, faith and religion two sides of me but also art, classical music and literature were of essential meaning – so many poems on poetry, classical music and painting.

Then Rosemarie and I have been very happily married for 57 years now. Impossible that a German and Jew could be so happily married so shortly after the war? I've written love poems for her, hundreds and hundreds over those 56 years, not only the love poems, as most are, of the first and often unfulfilling passion, but "love and marriage go together like a horse and carriage". Perhaps too prosaic for many poets?

When did I become a poet? My sister Lois wrote reasonably good poetry as an adolescent. I, only interested in sports until my Bar Mitzvah, a tournament tennis and table-tennis player, coached baseball and basketball teams, also soccer.

20

My sister asked whether I'd ever read Dostoyevsky. I'd only read John R. Tunis sports books and the sports section of the *New York Times* so I answered "in which sports was he active?" She said, rather condescendingly, "If you haven't read Dostoyevsky, you haven't lived." So I went to the library for the very first time and asked for a book by this Dostoyevsky. I received *Poor People*, his first book, that made him world famous. My mother shocked to see me reading and most especially a book about poor people said, "David, don't read that it will make you sad, unhappy – we, living in Scarsdale, weren't after all, poor people. From there it went quickly to my Tolstoy, Hardy and so on. In music it started with the hit parade, then *Lost in the Stars*, then the popular classics and with 15 or 16 my Haydn, Mozart, Schütz, Victoria … And then at Ann Arbor and NYU to my artists, most especially Giovanni Bellini, Van der Weyden, Georges de la Tour, Corot and Gauguin …

But it was Wallace Stevens' reading in the early 50s in the YMHA that set me off – he didn't read very well, but his 13 Ways of Looking at a Blackbird, Idea of Order at Key West, Two Letters (in *Poems Posthumous*), Peter Quince at the Clavier, The Snowman … and the excellent obituary in *Time* magazine plus the letter he answered some of my poems with compliments but "you must be your own hardest critic". That pre-determined my extremely self-critical way with a poem. Please don't believe that prolific means sloppy, for I'm extremely meticulous with each and every poem.

My poems are published in the order written and I'm way ahead of any counting … The poem is a dialogical process as everything in life. The words come to me not from me, and if they strike or possibly join-a-union then I become desparate, read long-winded poets like Paz to set me off – he's very good at odd times. Those poems need my critical mood-mind as much as I need its very specially chosen words – not the "magic words" of the romantics, but the cleansed words of Jaffin – Racine used only 500 words. My words too are a specially limited society, often used, but in newly-felt contexts.

O something very special: I have a terrible poetic memory. If I had a good one as presumably most poets, I'd write say one poem about a butterfly, and every time I see/saw a butterfly it would be that one, that poem. But I forget my poems, so each butter-fly, lizard, squirrel … is other-placed, other-mooded, other-worded, other-Jaffined. That's the main reason why I am most certainly the most prolific of all poets.

Shakespeare is the greatest of us: his sonnets live most from the fluency and density of his language. I advise all future poets to keep away from his influence and the poetic greatness of The Bible.

Yours truly
David Jaffin

P. S.: As a preacher the truth (Christ) should become straight-lined, timelessly so, but as a poet it's quite different. What interests me most are those contradictions which live deeply within all of us, not only in theory, but daily in the practice. And then the romantics have led me to those off-sided thoroughly poetic truths that mysteriously not knowing where that darkened path will lead us.

Dreams remain *(9)*

a) an enigma as
they're other
wise than a
play–back of

b) what's happen
ed but with inter
changeable
personae time
s and places

c) Why did they
come–out in
their own way
Does our brain
possess a

d) channel for

what–could–have–

been Or is a
master hand

directing a

e) warning for

dangers ahead
and even at

times a self–
satisfying

you–did–it–

f) just-right Dream

s seem to poss
ess a life-of–

their–own but
not just for

night–time

g) entertain

ment not real
ly ours but

most–certain
ly no-one–

elses If "life'

h) s nothing but

a dream" (Calder

on/Haydn) Why
are dream

s themselves
s but dis–simil

i) ar imitation

s of a life

that may have
been ours-for–

the-living-it.

If as modern (5)

a) *science has prov*

en what our

senses realize
if nothing o

b) *ther than the*

way we've been

receptive
ly aware of

their apparan
ces – that

c) *table there so*

solidly self–

sufficient
is "really"

nothing else
than emptied

d) spaces of in

betweened

matters less
what it "real

ly is" than
the way I've

e) known-it-to-

be Modern poet

ry may appear
for some more

like that table
less table.

The lessons *(5)*

a) we've learned

from life (if

any) are cer
tainly quite

b) different

from our own

grandchildren'
s Not only

have the chang
ing times left

c) their distinct

ive otherwise

ness but their
upbringing rare

ly signifies
similarit

d) ies with our

own Most import

ant to discov
er (if that'

s really possible)
what lessons

e) remain above

personal-prefer

ences and every
thing–else.

Nothing lessen *(3)*

a) s the true up-

and–about

self–deceptive
character of

b) life than lett

ing age pre–de

termine your
own mind–set

Sitting there
with others

c) similarly giv

ing-in to life'

s unduly felt
otherwise-pre

ference
s.

My New Year' (3)

a) s resolution

s never became

anything more
than that re

b) solutely hold

ing-on to the

so-much I
have Rosemarie

faith hope-for-
the-future friend

c) ships despite

my enigmatic

resolutely
personal–defi

ciencie
s.

He wrote him (2)

a) self daily out

of those self–

presenting
word–idea

s kept insist

b) ing on their

own poet to
take–care–of

their most de
termining

now–or–never
s.

These rain (3)

a) *s have lessen*

ed their con

tinuing appeal
as stories e

b) *ven as picares*

quely alived as

Pickwick Papers
or Mark Twain'

s Roughing It
loses their appro

c) *priating claim*

s on our first–

time energiz
ing off-balanc

ing acceptanc
es.

A tunnel (6)

a) darker than

its length

would imply
I took the

b) measure of

my child–like

resolve and
entered com

pletely alone

c) At first its

unexpected
warmth eased

my restraint
until I felt

d) emcompassed

by a depth

of an almost
personal welcom

ing but the

e) further I went

its length

seemed to be
increasing

out beyond my

f) will or even

ability for

turning back.

As a child *(2)*

a) he used to

count the star

s on a heaven
ly night encom

passing more
than even his

b) eyes could

seem until he

fell asleep
in the ease

of an untold
beyondness.

At first *(10)*

a) nothing but

this wordless

blank such a
precluding

b) darkness

that hinder

s that creat
ive where of

a most–alway

c) s adaptable

now Other poem
s even my own

may set this off
(not yet realiz

ing their desired
presence)

d) They call it

"priority
mail" sanction

e) ed (if only in

retrospect)
by its inbred

word–sense
Now the mind'

f) s almost at

the threshold

of its creat
ive there–be–

it but not

g) yet fully a

ware of its
time–involving

self-devising
theme It's like

h) waiting for the

train's next

stop yours if
rightfully track

ed Now fully

i) situated in

the morning'
s first–light–

bred oncoming
impulsing

s my own recept

j) ive there-be

ing nothing
more or less

than the poet
ically invoking

now.

Each new (3)

a) day heralding

its own self–

substantial
partially un

b) named but ex

actly number

ed to that
here-I-am noth

ing more or

c) less than my

light–spread
ing time-encom

passing pre
sence.

Only now

these distant
trees called–

out-of-the-
darkness to

the newly
discovered

height of
their time-sus

pending cause.

Once again *(3)*

a) referred to

"the father

of modern in
strumental

music" as

b) "papa" not

the father of
but a trivial

precursor
of Mozart and

Beethoven who

c) remained deep

ly dependent
on his so fresh

ly-original
form–creating

intuition.

Catching-up (8)

a) may also lead

to an overtak

ing as the
Spanish poetry

b) of the early

20th century

or Germany'
s post–war de

mocracy New
lands for both

c) realizing the

depth of that

unforeseen
self-inhabit

ing otherwise

d) ness Why has

East Germany
lagged-behind

still open–
land for author

e) itarian-nation

alism Because

it never de–
Nazified in

a democratic

f) sense replac

ing one ideolog
ical state

with another
Only time will

g) tell (as if

there hadn'
t been plenty

of time for
that) if it's

slowly ripen

h) ing for such

otherwise
soul-search

ings and those
most-difficult

first-steps.

Natural flower (2)

a) s hand-cut

for dispensible

domestic use
are at least

better than
artificial

b) flowers perpetu

ating a pretty

dead-sense of
touchless

time-invocat
ions.

Admitting (2)

a) one's mistake

s without the

usual scape-
goat's this or

that may be
come a most

b) certifying

judgment of

one's own
through-tell

ing charcter-
reach.

3 sermons *(3)*

a) in-a-row amened

our deeply bibli

cally-sourced
dean at just

b) the moment I

finalized

it for my
own-sake Such

time-expectan

c) cy is worthy

of a poetical
ly punctualiz

ing concrete-
sensibility.

22 Oak Lane *(5)*

a) Those attic

stairs off-
bounds for our

childrened
curiosity

b) now left va

cant before

the new owner
s move-in

to their lower

c) but seeming

ly better-
sourced confine

s I kept
wondering

d) why those up

stairs seem

ed to trans
cend our down-

stairs too

e) personally

activating
daily time-

holding
s.

It's the my (3)

a) sterious un

known the real

depth of the
ocean's bottom

b) less deep and

the untold spa

cious sky-
heights that

calls one's

c) poetically-

sensed blood
into an acti

vating appar
ent-display.

When a dog *(3)*

a) (the one he
chose) be
comes the
soul of per

sonally taking–

b) on its owner'
s most inti
mate affect

ions and if
it should die

where and what

c) would become
of his self-re
flecting fully

encompass
ing love-spell

s.

There's a (2)

a) time when par

ents should

realize enough
is enough

Middle-aged
children

b) can't be re

created in

the image of
one's own

liking
s.

That he so (5)

a) liberally

center-stage

should use
his excess

b) money to heed

his grandchild

ren to his own
self-securing

interests speak

c) s volumes of

his unrecorded
self-deceptive

appearance
s and it also

d) speaks against

his three-generat

ional family–
sense with one'

s children

e) battling on two

fronts That's
the real purpose

of his fam
ily-felt influen

cings.

No one could *(4)*

a) figure-him-

out the quiet

one a recluse
in a family

b) of big-talker

s Never seen

with an attract
ive woman and

most certain

c) ly not with o
therwise-orient
ed Asexual hard-
worker familied
only with his

d) university'
s (of all
things) base
ball team.

That moon (3)

a) momentarily
unseen its ti
dal power
s calling the

b) seas to their

primeval

ly distant shore
s Poeming these

reticent poem
s instinctive

c) ly to their

pre-assigned

reflective i
magining

s.

She's continu *(2)*

a) ally that most

necessary take–

charge kind of
a poet's wife

usually on the
right track

b) trained to cer

tain unknown

though time
ly-prevailing

landscaping
s.

Our friend *(2)*

a) s one by one

forsaking

this post–
Shakespear

ean stage of
our once to

b) getherness-

appearance

s now abandon
ing their fam

iliarly repeat
ed curtain-

calls.

Only a single *(11)*

a) messenger from

our long-depart

ed but short
ly-surviving

b) homestead

our wandering

though open-
eyed nephew

still in the

c) Greek tradition

of bringing us
up-to-date

of what's
long-since

d) (even though

most–surpris

ingly) dead–
and–gone

It's too late

e) now to recon

sider the
rights and

wrongs of
what I (fully

f) aware of the

consequence

s) left so
hastily behind

What's past

g) is past most

especially
in my brand-

new 2018 calen
dar The long-

h) view (most

opportune at

this New Year'
s appraisal

s) like slow

i) ly opening

a telescope
to its most

time-evoking
appearance

j) s which now
remain substan
tially so and
my unsteadied
eyes hardly ad

k) justing to what
remains all–
along hidden–
from–view.

Numbers either *(5)*

a) bring-to-mind
psalms in the
Judaic–Protest
ant tradition

b) *or Haydn's 104*

or even 107

symphonie
s (at least to

the finally
time-establish

c) *ing 150) What'*

s beyond must

stand complete
ly on-its-

own rights

d) *(the way I*

felt actual
ly pre-timed)

at my 80th birth
day leaving long

vistas behind

e) *and a most un*

certaining
(even timeless

ly evoking)
future.

Tomorrow' (4)

a) *s the long-a*

waited flight

to Florida
an ocean bet

b) *ween and an o*

therwise more

than climatic
change Not the

Hemingway'

c) s manly-muscul

ar Key West
drunkenness

but Wallace
Stevens' "Idea

d) of (an) Order"

as mysterious

ly-receptive
time-unfolding

wave-length
ed.

If we've (3)

a) failed to convey

cultural value

s to our son
It's his pro

b) blem now not

ours But such

a strict
denial im

plies a still
lingering adoles

c) cent rebellion

so character

istic of a fam
ily-question

ing Jaffines
que tradition.

It remind *(3)*

a) s of washing

one's tear

s away This
winter but

still penetrat

b) ing sun's re

lease of the
night's most in

tensive rain
s from the

face of its

c) untimely and

most-friendly-
warmthed tree'

s withholding-
appearance

s.

That tempor *(3)*

a) ary time-re

claiming un

ease before a
long-distant

b) flight perhap

s hardly other

wise than the
migrating

birds practis
ing their ready–

c) to-start

mountainous

ly urging
autumnal–

shadow
ings.

Waiting-to- *(4)*

a) be-discovered

may well charact

erize Pre–Colum
bian America

b) Even-more-so

the Hawaii of

its unknown
white war–god'

s coming on

c) his chosen cele

brating day
Why should I

complain as
Schubert or E

d) mily D. of my

self–inhabit

ing poetically
hermetic i

solation.

He's still *(2)*

a) rounding that

race-track

completely a
lone left be

hind all poten

b) tial competit

ors imagin
ing such a

uniquely-pro
lific poetic-

rival.

c) "Strike when

the iron's
hot" but this

one seems al
most permanent

ly so he's
striking the

poetical
warmth out

of it's time-
and-again.

Have it *(6)*

a) your way or

have it mine

Whatever
happened histor

ically or per
sonally continue

b) s to live its

own this way

or that with
no self-certain

ties left

c) What's general

ly accepted as
Guido Reni'

s highly roman
tic statued ap

d) pearance may

also in differ

ing times and
artistical

ly visual–

e) lengths become

taken–down from
its once ex

alted pedestal
Whereas other

f) s as Vermeer

and Georges de

la Tour have
risen to take

their vacantly
appointed place

g) Times tell their

own but limited

truths not
always lasting

ly-so.

Does the (4)

    a) change of lin

    guistic express

    iveness between
    romantic and

    b) modern also in

    dicate a radi

    cal aesthetic
    otherwise

    ness Maybe so

c) but a post-ro

mantic mood–en
ticing lyricism

may remain in
need of a

d) newly-realized

classically–

exacting
word–sense.

He tried his *(3)*

a) best to avoid

those personal

road–repetit
ive incision

s that leave

b) even the fin

est of cars
stop-bound

But with his
usual mounting

emotional thrust

c) himself right in

to that no-man
s land with

little chance
of a time-even

ing return.

Florida

These field

s so heavy with
fog as if in

need of a lone
ly escape from

winter's sleep
or perhaps they'

re concealing
whatever may

seem invisibly
low-levelled.

This airport'

> s so many dir
> ectioned shadow
>
> ing unseen des
> tinations
>
> that sitting
> still seems
>
> as an inappro
> priate defiance
>
> of the rules-
> of-the-game.

So many win

> dows here look
> ing higher than
>
> one's own daily
> use smalled–
>
> him-down to a
> littleness
>
> hold of a chair
> that seemed ade
>
> quately pre-es
> tablish
>
> ed.

That granite

    ring's intens
    ing the hard-

    coloring–flash
    of its momen

    tary light–
    sensed appeal

    s.

Why have so (3)

    a) few that necess

    ary feel for

    poetic sensi
    bility whereas

    b) music and art

    seem such more

    accessibly
    sensed Poetry

    has them both

c) but it may

be the word
that remain

s intricate
ly more demand

ing.

Some person

s tower at such
an unspeakable

height that it
becomes quite

difficult for
me (one of the

self-satisfying
lesser ones)

to really size-
them-up.

Language (4)

a) is a most mis-

used tool per

haps because
it's so often

b) taken-for-grant

ed that it

misses-the-mark
of what it

really want

c) s to convey

Isn't that per
haps words to

day are like
jewelled nugget

d) s one must

dig through lev

els of dross to
reactivate

their still
shiny presence.

Philosopher (2)

a) s may question

the real sense

of words their
actual meaning

whereas poet
s allow those

b) self-same word

s to explore

what remain
s untouchably

inexpress
ible.

Mindless

poetry awakens
the senses

but if poetry
becomes too

mindful it may
not recognize

itself at all.

Do we remain

continually
in need of those

inexplicable
images to satis

fy the most pur
poseful realm

of poetry's
raison d'être.

Alone on the

lake our boat

remained as
companion

able as those
softly wave-e

choing-
s.

Do we leave (3)

a) what's so mean

ingfully learn

ed behind us
(those long

rows of most

b) ly used book

s on our self–
securing

shelves) Or
have they be

come so much

c) a part of us

that we seem
to have forgott

en them alto
gether.

Greenland'

s not green
but white but

if you re
name it might

all melt–away
into the green

of your most
reveried

dream
s.

For Viktor (3)

a) Frankl there

were no red-

lines All
could find sense

b) and meaning

There was also

a never-too-
late Frankl was

saintly Few of

c) us are made

of such compass
ion even for

our enemie
s.

Those who con *(2)*

> *a) tinually watch*

> trivial T. V.

> movies will be
> come in time

> trivial them

> *b) selves Or per*

> haps they so
> enjoy them for

> the same self–
> perpetuating

> reason.

Can you see *(2)*

> *a) the cold as in*

> visible as the

> wind but it
> leaves its

> mark as well
> feels a numb

b) ness a deaden

ing of the

blood stream
s to their un

touchably
bared–down ori

gins.

All that in (2)

a) a 50 degree

Floridian

morning's
denial Setting–

up his usual
umbrellas

b) as small child

ren all lined–

up for rows
of expectant

class–route
s.

It *has-to-be-*

done that do
or die command

ing voice as a
sergeant with

his reticent
troop's forward-

march time-dis
tinguishing

causality.

Time-sharing (2)

a) here with main

ly mid-western

ers gets-the-most
out-of-the-

rest-of-your-

b) life swim sun

and golf main
ly time-absorb

ing pre-diagnos
tic interest

s.

Mirroring *(2)*

a) another per

son looking

back at you'
re at least

two person
s faintly a

b) ware of that

differing

Why mirror at
all realizing

the unity of
your self–dis

guising I am.

If America' *(3)*

a) s a melting-pot

it's melting

what's substan
tially away or

b) it was never

really meant

that way from
its Virginia and

Massachusett

c) s origining

an experiment
in an other

wise divisive
ness.

If poetry' (6)

a) s another way

of trying to

understand
what will al

b) ways remain enig

matic then it

should remain
as an insolu

ble mystery of

c) beauty's self-

deceptive o
therwise appar

encie
s Why try to

d) resolve what

seems at con

tradictory
ends of your

at least two–

e) wise personal

expressive
ness They'll re

main as long as
poetry's in

f) such self-suffi

cient need of

an explicitly
wording–it–

just–right.

It's warming

today and those
distances open

ing-out invis
ible perspect

ives of once
realized time–

inherent silen
ces.

Hide and Seek *(2)*

   a) an always favor

   ite children'

   s game for
   life's continu

   al identity-
   change until

   b) you're found-

   out or finding

   those hidden
   darknesses'

   increasing
   self-establish

   ing.

Low-tide *(2)*

   a) as those depthed

   slow-movement

   s of Haydn space-
   expressive

   not as with
   Beethoven dramatic

b) ally self-ap

parent but inward

ly silenced as
illusive as per

soned shadow
ings.

Sands as (2)

a) light as morn

ing's first un

veiling presen
ce as if dark

ness itself'

b) s but a tenta

tive illusion
of man's self–

calling tragic
appearance

s.

Precision

itself's but a
word-defining

means for an
allusive pre-

understand
ing of what

will always
remain change

ably uncertain
ed.

Tiny child

dren's first
run-stepping

sand's excita
bility but then

the apparent
more lasting

taste of stand
ing full-stop.

Fat boys as

Billy Schreiber
early marked–

off as no way
of moving such

a body-full ele
gantly.

Pelican'

s just glid
ing by out–

reaching the
spacious

length of
their wing's

extending time-
view.

At this win

dowed–distance
the waves voice

fully unheard
softly caress

ing the shore'
s receptive

but still self–
withholding

response.

Today Florida' *(2)*

a) s once again

timely warming–

up to its pre–
establish

ing presence
The palms soft

b) ly wind-comply

ing femininely

attuned to their
unseen but light

ly heard phras
ings.

Some person *(5)*

a) s mostly home–

oriented women

find it diffi
cult to live

b) even for a

short-time out

of the context
of the familiar

has become

c) whether reali

zed or not their
modus vivendi

They measure
the otherwise-ex

d) perienced on

what's become

so much a part
of their very-

being They domest

e) icate the society

itself in their
own self-satis

fying image.

I don't real (4)

a) ly know how

these time-shar

ing apartment
s as ours per

sonally realize

b) their own sense

of being occup
ied a week here

or two and
then another

c) family moves in

It's more like

Beethoven's
way never long

in a single
self-situat

d) ing place But

what becomes of

it as some per
sons most alway

s left-behind.

Everything (4)

   a) done that has

to be done

what still ...
a nagging feel

ing of what

b) more for life

continually
confronts

that so easily
self–fulfill

c) ing off-balanc

ing our so

steadily self–
satisfying

finishing–
ups And if

d) it didn't bore

dom would

slowly overtake
our most initiat

ing resolve.

When Florida (3)

  a) *becomes its so-*

  called "real self"

  again and the
  January sun

  b) *though still*

  lacking its

  heightened
  time–appeals

  an intensing
  heat penetrat

  c) *ing even the*

  mind's most se

  clusively hidd
  en realm

  s.

A little

boy with a big
coloring ball

rounding him
self out as

Columbus to a
previously

undiscover
ed world-view.

Viktor Frankl' (4)

a) s real authority

however great

ly enchanced by
his professor

b) ships especial

ly self-revealing

those 4 concen
tration camp

s failed to

c) take the human

ity out of
his God–fear

ing Judaic self–
resilient stand

d) ing-up to evil

at its most

devastating
source.

Is the past *(4)*

a) simply past

lacking a signi

ficant future
relevance

b) or does it

continue to

realize itself
often in the

most unsuspect
ed forms For

c) some it still

haunts their

daily present
raison d'être

For others it
may become as

d) with Viktor

Frankl an ex

ample for the
future orient

ation of o
thers.

When the (2)

a) *tide's coming-*

in there's an

instinctive
pull some

where near the

b) *heart's sound-*

regions out to
sea holding-

tight for safe-
securing

s.

This beach (2)

a) *continues to re*

define the

length of my
sea–scaping

thoughts as
those tide

b) s coming in

or out and

the moon's light–
reclaiming and

still mysterious
awakening

s.

These wind-

blown cloud
s curiously

shaping what
seems time

lessly unre
solving while

it messages its
still unrelent

ing but unknown
source.

Should we (2)

a) write this lang

uage anew fresh

ly envision
ing our person

ally refining
perspective

b) as a shell

now opened to

the sea's in
creasingly

voiced tidal–
advance

s.

Can we real *(3)*

a) ly be certain

we've chosen

the right path
barely signify

ing its way in

b) to the wood'

s darkening
enclosure

s No signs
left even the

previous foot

c) steps no longer

marking–out
their decisive

ly singular en
compassing

s.

One can't *(3)*

a) poem it simply

this way or that

according to
our own change

b) able sensibilit

ies It must

direction our
hesitant appro

val and if
that certainty

c) *fails the poem'*

s failed too

of its most
necessary

form-decisive
raison d'être.

How much of (2)

a) *what we've learn*

ed remains as

flesh to the
bones of our

self-certified
identity-cause

b) *And who's to*

say that's my

own genuine
self-being

and not simply
an unauthoriz

ed imitation.

How often (3)

a) do we sense

that something'

s missing It
may be an im

b) portant item

we've failed

to pack but
it can also

be an empti

c) ness in our

own self-deceiv
ing identity-ap

parencie
s.

An always

being there
when you need

him most like
a signifying

ring that doesn'
t as my wedd

ing-gold loosen
in that sea

of lost-appear
ances.

To the one- (5)

a) sided memory of

my father For

some children
become a part

b) of their own

time-extending

person (often
only the name

will suffice)

c) For others

they're our
own means of

creating what'
s continual

d) ly pursuing

its own scarce

ly realizing
identity-cause

as a continu

e) ing burden for

our self-per
petuating sanct

ification.

If the poem (4)

a) decides to

write you

There's no
way I know of

b) avoiding its

most necessary

claims It grasp
s on your own

self-sufficience
s.

c) It offers what

you're most lack
ing the flesh

and blood of its
very-being and

d) then it command

s in a most per

sistent way
write–me–out.

Does the sea *(3)*

a) emerge out of

this declining

darkness as
some of the

b) ancient gods

and goddesses

Or is this on
coming morning

but lighten

c) ing the depth

of your own
self–precluding

silence
s.

These palms *(3)*

a) have become

nothing more

than the wind'
s soft

b) ening quest of

Florida's youth

ful calling
s escpecially

for mid–western
er's retiring

c) *from life's o*

therwise pro

tracting identi
ty-cause

s.

Rosemarie

the self-perpet
uating love-of–

my-life's also
the muse of

my better-self
poeming itself

out's together
ness from that

self-fulfill
ing source.

Plained (3)

a) *Plain living*

plain good

common–sense
thinking a

plain daily-
used language

b) nothing poet

ic left ex

cept those
wind-folding

fields of grain

c) and the untold

distance
s they're

time-expand
ing.

The sound of

horse-shoes
clashing asson

ant steadied–
hold of strength

ening point–
blank reassur

ances.

It's those (2)

a) lightly-sensed

waves contin

ually soften
ing my alway

s impression

b) ed touched-

feelings for
the sand's

time–waiting
receptiv

ity.

Advice to Alena at 16 (3)

a) When your i

maginings

actually ex
ceed what'

s seen or

b) heard you're

either an en
thusiast or

creative in
your own-right

Better to tone-

c) down such ex

pectation
s and let your

mind rehearse
its own craftful

know-hows.

This Floridian *(3)*

a) beach now peopled-

blossoming all

the umbrella
s upstanding

b) your vacation

ed feeling

s own privileg
ed Sunday-best

pleasuring

c) sun-lit if less

substantial
instinctual

uplifting
s.

Riding the *(2)*

a) waves in is

like letting

the tidal-flow
fully immerse

you in its
fundamental

word-sense.

b) At sunset

the precluding
silences spread

ing-out their
time-immersing

shadowing
s.

Tropical (2)

a) nights when the

dark become

s so pervasive
that even one'

s own shadow
s lose the

b) lengthened

depth of their

distinguish
ing identity-

cause.

Feet-find

ing for the tin
iest of tots

as the small
est of birds

here propell
ing to the

highest gear
of relinquish

ing their own
body's forget

fulness.

In this abbrev (5)

a) iating world of

rarely full-ex

pressiveness
Perhaps only

b) the poetical

ly redefining

word–claim
s may save us

from this once

c) Shakespear

ean linguist
ic dense-ap

proval
s If imagin

d) ing currents a

depth of irre

trievably
sourced word–

swells then
it's fashion

e) ed with unfath

omed truths

even beyond
the Rankean

as it real
ly became time–

securing.

Cross-word (2)

a) *puzzles most*

always blacken-

out what's not
to be resolved

and so do those
political and

b) *even personal*

opportuned

what's not in
their pre-conceiv

ed raison-
d'être.

The fogs are (2)

a) *in obscuring*

the now as

if lost into
a deeply for

gotten it–could–
have-been until

122

b) the sun's re

awakened high-

lighting time'
s uncertain

ed self-reveal
ings.

Florida' *(2)*

a) s in no way

Ponce-de-León's

Garden of Youth
but more a vast

old-age home
d in the wish

b) ful thinking

s of a soft

and leisurely
post-retire

ment health-
spa.

Red and blue (2)

a) or blue and grey

America remain

s a divided
nation between

white and color
ed North and

b) South rich and

poor and what

ever else den
ies the myth of

its once so-
called melting-

pot oneness.

Why or when (5)

a) did I become a

poet hard-to-

know I think
it's more like

ly the poem
s decided to in

b) habit me It

was their choice

for whatever
reason ask them

still being

c) duly written-

out If you
concentrate

your mind and

d) senses to a

no–wheres–but–
now the poem

has already
been called

until it begin

e) s asking you

however certain
ing by your

own name's
sake.

An old-age- *(2)*

a) home without

the enlivening

presence of
dogs and cat

s and other
possible ani

b) mals has resign

ed its inhabi

tants to a self–
perpetuating

all–inclusive
boredom.

Those who seek-

  out the presence
  of glass–bowled

  fish are usual
  ly fully–attun

  ed to the color
  ing–aesthetic

  s of a sound
  less–poetiz

  ing.

Those in any (2)

  a) sport who sit-

  out the game

  on a harden
  ed bench re

  main suspend
  ing between

  b) an actively o

  therwise know–

  how and a
  spectator'

  s pre–determin
  ing judgment.

That fat boy (2)

a) of pre-school

age unease

s me because
with several

even younger
siblings he'

b) s been neglect

ed to his

(perhaps evil)
own imagining

impulse
s.

Horse-shoe

s fascinate
me especial

ly because of
that eyed-pre

cision so much
a part of my

poetically
certained

there-being.

Life may (3)

a) deny most any

obstacle

Just visual
ize those de

b) sert cactus

flowers or

those strange
deep-darkness

es' espoused fish-
like creature

c) s and yet we

daily take it

(life) so-
much-for-grant

ed.

It's only

the dialoguing
eye that real

izes what I'
ve seen has

also been
looking straight-

through my
self-reveal

ing precept
ions.

"He passed a(2)

a) way" – which

way "He's no

longer here" –
where is he

then Death's
the unanswered

b) question and

will always re

main so in its
secretly in

visible domain.

Trumpism (5)

a) *Those non-swimm*
ers who jump
in the lake
may of necess

b) *ity learn to*
swim for their
life but even
seek-out deep
waters as if it's

c) *their own pre-*
conceived al
ways available
landing-place

d) Those who rare

ly apologize

for their own
mistakes but

counter–punch
instead become

e) offensive for

all who value

good behavior
as a character–

based criteria.

We were walk (2)

a) ing these sand

s yesterday

in the late
afternoon

or were they
walking us

b) into their

own solely

cherished re
ceding–distan

ces.

For George *(2)*

a) Those gifted

with a creative

original mind
should realize

it's on loan
if wrongly us

b) ed it could

be taken a

way without
your realiz

ing when or e
ven why.

Friendship

as anything
else of real

intrinsic
value must be

cultivated or
else it may

take-a-distan
ce to its in

itial raison-
d'être.

Those usual

ly suspicious
of others may

well be hiding
something

from their own
hardly recogniz

able past.

Some palm (2)

a) s as person

s I've known

hardly able
to straight–

line to an up

b) right posture

they lyrical
ly curve their

way to a multi-
leafed express

iveness.

These cloud *(3)*

a) s seem to be

breeding their

own cause as
if risen from

b) the sea column

s of darkly

brooding re
membrance

s of ancient
gods and goddess

c) es re-establish

ing their realm

s of sea–bound
eternitie

s.

Even for a (2)

a) word-resourced

but aging poet

they (the necess
ary words) may

refuse their
most timely pre

b) sence as the

queen in the

biblical book
of Esther dead–

blanked for fu
ture denial.

If parent *(6)*

a) s and their

grown children

were asked
what they re

b) member best

of their child

hood upbring
ing they'll

most alway

c) s answer quite

differently
not only be

cause their
perspective

d) s remained o

therwise but

also because
the children

had begun to

e) assume their own

identity often
at their

parent's attempt

f) (often uncon

sciously) to pre

form their own
children.

Strangely

appearing these
long-bearded

workmen hatted
too in a most

dissembling
way of mask

ing their hand-
felt daily call

ings.

Tunnels led

George and my
self into

those similar
darkly-feared

self-encompass
ing death-pre

monition
s.

Well-chosen *(2)*

a) compelling com

parisons are

like such o
ther-sourced

sisters find
ing themselve

b) s sitting under

a tree shadow

ing a most
similar mood-

expressive
ness.

Strange *(4)*

a) stoned-format

ions in the

midst of the
desert as watch

b) towers witness

ing what's be

come lifeless
ly untold Build

ing castles in

c) the sand with a

child-like care
ful even histor

ical devotion
is like medieval

d) Jews burying

their lonesome

treasure to the
oncoming blood-a

rousing sacrifi
cial-death.

When the con (3)

    a) stant use of

    abbreviation

    s also abbre
    viates those

    b) who can deciph

    er such a hidd

    en expressive
    ness Then it'

    s about–time
    to stand–up

    c) for the fully-

    sourced lang
    uage of a Shakes

    peare and Mil
    ton.

One continue (6)

a) s to daily

write numerous

poems as proof
to oneself of

b) still remain

ing a poet

It's like kiss
ing one's wife

repeatedly re

c) assuring her

receptive I
love-you-too

response Are
such naturally

d) sent occuren

ces as the hea

venly changea
bilities of

clouds or tree

e) s or flower

s most always
direction

ed towards hea
ven The Lord'

f) s way of saying

I still re

main so en
gaged for

you.

This late

morning's palm'
s blurred and

darkened re
flection

while still re
maining trans

parent as if
wind-sensing

an alternate
raison d'être.

Can one be *(2)*

a) written-out

too much with

nothing more
to see feel

think reflect
not even those

b) tidal flow

s still immens

ing you in
their stream

of creative-ex
pressiveness.

It's too (2)

a) cool these day

s even for

tropical bird
s The sand

s are emptied
and only these

b) vacant wind

s keep recall

ing their per
sistent most-pre

vailing time-ex
posure

s.

These palm (3)

a) s appear to

have been grow

thed out of
stone in de

b) fiance of

their once

speechless
presence

They lengthen

c) a slender

height of de
sirably leaf

ful imagining
s.

Insect *(3)*

a) s scarcely in

habiting our

more northern
climbs while

b) here the trop

ical bird

s reduced to
a lonely few

Something
feels empty

c) now right-

down to our

own existen
cial life–

base.

It's hard to

be prolific
if you've

little to say
and those real

ly gifted u
sually need

more to express
than they them

selves can
realize why.

In a good *(4)*

> *a) marriage there'*
> s nothing left
> to be measur
> ed-out What

> *b) I've done for*
> you contra
> what you've
> done for me
> We've become

> *c) a singular-*
> we and if
> not the marr
> iage itself
> will continual

d) ly be quest

ioning its own

uncertained
raison d'être.

If a sermon

doesn't question
"Where do we

come from What
are we and Where'

s our life's
end-station"

then it isn'
t preaching

the-living-
word-of-Christ.

Some Christian (4)

a) s believe they'

ve the finaliz

ed ticket mark
ed with the

b) blood of the

cross for hea

venly sancitude
s But Jesus as

He himself

c) may envision it

otherwise
as if blind–

folded to
their very

d) self-confirm

ing ladder

ed height
s.

He needed (3)

a) a wife who

would as his

mother stand–
up even again

b) st his usual

ly self-preclud

ing sense of
right and wrong

Marriage as a
vitally self-en

c) hancing boxing-

match though

without those
last round'

s knock-out
s.

Don't ever *(9)*

a) trust the un

proven taste

of others in
food culture

b) or whatnot

I've often dis

covered as with
Borges poets

similar to my

c) own express

iveness but
with views of

other poet
s diametrical

d) *ly opposed to*

them And then

friends recom
mending this

or that rest

e) *aurant "you*

try-it-out"

And often we'
ve gone home

f) *with a much-*

lessened-wallet

and a still
under-nourished

appetite Even

g) our own taste

s can be most
changeable

without our
fully realiz

h) ing why Popular

taste as those

Nobel prizes
for literature

rarely satis

i) fying our own

otherwise
cultivated

sense-for-
beauty.

Restless

palms leaving
an unease re

flective feel
ing on the

windows of
their wind-per

petuating
s.

If "there are (2)

a) no words for

it"'s unbeliev

able Allan
may then have

been mysterious
ly touched with

b) what remain

s hidden some

where beyond
reach of his

actually now
and where.

When Daryl (2)

    a) preaches there'

s no–way–out

to stop list
ening to think–

up excuses for

    b) your everyday

behavior
He chairs you

to an inescap
able attentive

ness.

If (as I've (4)

    a) always felt)

my poems are

better than
me because

b) they've noth

ing to conceal

because they'
ve cleansed

my everyday

c) usage Those who

take to them
often despite

my so-called
self have tak

d) en to the bett

er part of

my kaleido
scopic per

spective
s.

Daryl *(5)*

a) preaches me

back to what

once dominated
my personal

b) sense-of-call

ing to Jesus

the Jew in post–
Holocaust Ger

many That hasn'

c) t really chang

ed somewhere
depthed in those

most interior
levels of my

d) very-being

But now I've

become as orig
inally sourced

the poet of His

e) creational

beautifying
resource

s.

She'd most *(5)*

a) probably been

a waitress her

entire life
Such work had

b) become a call

ing for her e

ven in her
pre-retire

ment age a

c) sense of happ

ily satisfy
ing the wishes

of other
s Each year

d) after church we

seated ourselve

s in close
range to her

pre-given
territorial

e) claims No one

impeded there

her mark
ed–out pleas

uring appeal
s.

Blank page *(4)*

a) s remain for

me as an empty

canvas for a
Charles Seliger

b) a pre-design

ed calling as

the moon's mag
netic pull on

sleep–walker

c) s can't deny

it would be
like forgett

ing the name
of your old

est and dear

d) est friend

word-it-out
paint-it-in

There's no o
ther recourse

when such a

e) calling's in

habiting those
vacant space

s of your pre-
worded identity-

cause.

Barry (6)

a) He spent time

in prison mis-

using other
people's money

b) Think of that

as you will

but for him
(a cousin and

my eldest sis

c) ter's contempor

ary) I remem
ber two meeting

s so complement
ary in the

d) train when he

a so-called

successful law
yer bragged how

he k. o. ed each
and every oppon

e) ent and then

at my mother'

s 100th birthday
party he open

ly and simply
referred to him

f) self as "the

black sheep in

the family" My
Christian heart

went out to
him then and

there.

I used to (3)

a) *believe her*

stories until

twice in a
short time–

b) *spell those*

mostly involv

ed said they
weren't true

Perhaps her
story telling

c) *had become a*

means of remem

bering what
hadn't happen

ed.

It's hard (3)

> *a) to be certain*
>
> whether these
>
> long corridor
> s lengthen
>
>
> *b) or shorten*
>
> my view espec
>
> ially when
> they start mov
>
> ing in oppos
>
>
> *c) ite direction*
>
> s to my–own–
> way–out of an
>
> increasing
> dilemma.

He had that *(2)*

a) getting-down-to-

business look

hair shortly
fashion

ed through his
phrasing word–style

b) Dressed most ap

propriately

the his dollar–
and-cent stead

ied impression.

Poems start

ing-out on the
wrong foot

Must be re–balan
ced back to a

wholesome
view of a not

necessary
time-invoking

word–spell.

Those who

continually
express them

selves in super
latives are

really mirror
ing their own

smallness of
word-competen

cy.

For Neil (2)

a) It's those

sudden over

coming pain
s that remind

us of who-we-

b) are and what

we aren't re
linquishing

our grasp of
this so imper

manent life-
scope.

"She ain't (2)

a) *what she used-*
to-be" Are we

ever thered
to a full–

stop Time's

b) *actually tell*
ing us its
own and our

so private
ly otherwise

ness.

Gottfried

Benn's strange
ly-sourced ar

chaic imagery
reminds of a

world that
never could–

have-been only
its word-trans

cending appar
ence.

Some of

those upflight
ing gulls seem

to be showing–
off especial

ly while glid
ing their air–

suspending sup
eriority.

Who's telling *(2)*

a) *"the truth the*

whole truth and

nothing but
the truth" if

there's no sub
stantial proof

b) *at either end*

Who's concealing

his side–to–the–
story best most

convincing
ly intact.

Imagine *(5)*

a) him pacing the

train station

back and forth
as if overcom

b) ing a most im

portant decis

ion weighing
those short and

long-term-effect

c) s of his as

yet undecid
ing choice Has

he become that
not yet oncom

d) ing train track

ed to the u

sual reconsider
ed time-length

s.

Taking one (3)

a) self too serious

ly a repetitive

cause for re
curring death–

b) fears A light

er step and a

casually recept
ive mind

c) may help di

minish those o

vercoming
time-compell

ing darkness
es.

How much be *(2)*

a) comes genuine

ly self-reveal

ing through
the dialoguing

response of
friend and foe

b) alike Or would

such mirroring

one's own re
flective duali

ties become a
more self-se

curing source.

His over *(2)*

a) lengthening

bearded self-
presence remind

s of the squir
rel's elongat

ing tail
s them even

b) beyond the

activating

distances of
a branch–for–

branch resumé.

One thing

he couldn't
write-off

that recurring
pained its own

self-response
decisively

more.

Some poem

s must become
resigned to

"getting-out-
of-hand" (poor

ly crafted)
while other

s lack the
necessary

mood-sensibil
ities.

Talk-show (2)

a) s talking-out

an issue down

to its very-
existencial

ground-base

b) (rarely) justi

fied for their
ever-repetitive

change of self-
assuming direct

ions.

Age continu

ally grows-on–
us often unob

served its
time–securing

pre–establish
ing impending

sourced-end.

These poem

s wave–recept
ive low–tidal

flatly sand–
horizoned

but an unbro
ken time–re

claiming dis
tancing.

Something (3)

a) missing as at

Lake Erie year

s back no
swimming those

b) polluted water

s But here–

and–now the
most beautify

ing of tropi

c) cal birds left

an emptiness
of their color

ed–shadowing
s behind.

More false- *(2)*

a) starts then

fully resourc

ed poems to
day leaving me

as an empty–
handed beggar

b) without even

the necessary

tin-cup collect
ing those few

worn-down face
less coin

s.

Afraid

of his instinct
ual up-start

s he learned
to distance

himself from
what could off-

set his more
than residual

timed-plann
ing.

Some of (2)

a) these softly

flowing palm

s leave an im
pression of

familiar
ity as if

b) they'd been

so voiced

through the
sky's most

timely blue–
searching

s.

Only a whiff

of clouds whis
pering transpar

ent flight–call
ings.

Lost in

thought beyond
the cloud'

s immersing
horizon could

n't find his
way back to

a safely secur
ing time–

hold.

The vastness

of this Flori
dian cloud-ful

filling day
left him with

that epic feel
ing of an

almost over
whelming time-

spell.

One could

call it a
creative urge

or better yet
let that "it"

redefine its
increasing

sense for
word-stream

ed effectiv
ity.

For Rosemarie *(2)*

a) those moment

s when our

eyes meet not
mid-way but in

fusing a unif
ied identity–

c) claim as you

fashioned your

usually recept
ive eyes in

to a time-re
claiming re

sonance.

Early enough *(3)*

a) in the morning

not a soul

in sight (as
if souls could

b) be seen) or

even a person

ed flesh and
blood's time

ful response

c) The sea quiet

ed-down from
its off unsub

dued persist
ent–question

ings.

Inside-out (2)

a) Don't judge

persons from

their look
s may turn–

you–off or
measured in

b) side/out of

what still re

mains discord
ant self–ap

parent.

Guardian *(3)*

a) Angels If there

really are

such then Rose
marie must

b) have signed-

up to take

good care of
this minister

turned poet

c) ically neither

here nor there
most seldom

approachable
initiative

s.

Can these

cool early morn
ing time-settl

ing winds e
voke truly Flori

dian cloud-en
compassing

spacious-imag
ining

s.

Are these

thin-lined
palms grace

fully wind-ex
posing at the

top of such
a lengthly

time-extend
ing measur

ing pole.

If he so (2)

a) carefully chose

just the ideally

self–express
ive words for

what he's mo
mentarily

b) sensed-seen

Could another

poet of say e
qual quality

be enabled to
landscape it

otherwise.

If swimming (3)

a) activates your

hidden strength

even in the
enclosure

b) s of this

small-sized

pool you may
actually be

imitating

c) wild animal'

s response to
their caged–

in self-suffi
cience

s.

Some poet *(2)*

a) s may feel

the need to

re-language
its lost ex

pressive
ness perhaps

b) life itself

s become rout
ined to a

word–like in
difference.

Low tides

may realize
one's own

softened sen
sibililtie

s back to
the sea's im

mensing tide
ful quieting

s.

That sudden

surge of pro
mising expectat

ions left him
inescapably

teen–aged to
those lost

vistas of now
however–much

ed never–more.

Meeting (2)

a) s between child

ren of SS murder

ers and those
of their life–

spared victim
s may have dis

b) covered the

familiar

ing unreconcil
ing presence

of a past-con
tinuity.

Translation (2)

a) s however necess

ary leave me

with the feel
of crossing a

bridge between
what's left–

b) *behind and*

what's still a

head though
mostly primed

mid-air.

The last (ing) (2)

a) *word Is it the*

poet or the

poem itself
that retain

s the last
(ing) word a

b) *gainst critic*

s otherwise

readers and
his own poem

ed sensibil
ity.

Some people

down here are
so over-weight

ed that I get
such a heavy

feeling simply
looking at

their time-ex
posing fat

nesses.

Good Intent (3)

a) ions Fear of

heights and

a direction
less means

of so easily

b) getting lost

that I began
to wonder

where that
home-stretch

had so inex

c) cusably

been hiding-
out from my

well-intent
ioned know-

how.

2nd Commandment *(Moses) (2)*

a) Are most child

ren brought–

up to a self–
sufficient

identity–cause
Or have their

parents usual

b) ly unsuccess

fully tried to
bring-them-down

to the image of
parental wish

ful thinking
s.

For men be (6)

  a) ing moved-to-

  tears may signi

  fy a state of
  exhaustion

  b) or even a wo

  manly-like e

  motional weak
  ness Or on-the-

  other-hand reveal

  c) ing an unusual

  depth of express
  ive receptiv

  ity Those who
  "carry their

d) hearts on their

shirt–sleeve

s" may become
in need of an

extra dose of

e) strengthen

ing vitamin
s whereas

those unable
to cry at the

f) death of their

beloved wife or

mother may
seem heartless

ly unemotional
ly-depthed.

Looking-out

at the sea
may refeel a

kind of ti
dal-response

to one's contin
ually change

able life-ex
perience

s.

Despite the (3)

a) artificial

ity of a doctor'

s waiting room
or a bank'

b) s so sensed

pleasing swing–

time music
Can one still

remain aware

c) of the beyond

ness of o
ther times and

place's vastly
living–presen

ce.

Those who (2)

a) harbor new shore

s as Gauguin

may discover
the pre-given

landscaping'

b) s awakened from

one's own
darkly withhold

ing identity-
claim

s.

A grand Ameri (3)

a) can-sized museum

in Sarasota Flor

ida's almost 20
rooms filled

b) with 2nd and 3rd

rate quality

painting
s (that Tit

ian and Frans

c) Hals must have

been secretly
brought-in)

through the
"not so quality"

backdoor.

For Corinne and Tom (4)

a) *Some friend*

ships continue

to grow as
crops from a

fertile land

b) *simply through*

the rewarding
pleasured ex

perience
s in a famil

c) *iarity of per*

soned togeth

erness while
carefully a

voiding those

d) remaining still

untouchable
theme

s.

As my poetry'

s the–better–
side–of–self

Those who take–
to–it more like

ly to welcome
my oft unpreach

er–like ambig
uitie

s.

For many

a Jew'll alway
s remain a Jew

no matter what
religion pro

fession or the
like Why then

try to hide
from The Lord'

s unearned
chosenness.

Getting over

filled with word
s until that

overflow as a
cross-word puzzle

securing a se
lective choice

of an alway
s self-intend

ing caused-
finality.

For Corinne (3)

a) Did Shakespeare

retire to his

hometown be
cause he'd noth

ing more to

b) say and/or be

cause he felt
a lack of creat

ive-urge and/or
because he'd

c) grown suspic

ious of the di

minishing qual
ity of much of

his later work.

Does the so (2)

a) personal relation

with even Shakes

peare's minor
character

b) s indicate that

human behavior

(however time
and national

even class

c) changeabil

ity) still re
veals basically

curtained psycho
logical truism

s.

Does Shakes *(3)*

a) peare's life-long

continuing inter

est in the
theatre indi

cate that des

b) spite the great

ness of many of
his sonnets and

their uniquely
depthed language

imply his belief

c) that poetry'

s a still more
limited ex

pressive-
mean

s.

If we "Anglo- *(3)*

a) Saxons" continue

to measure the

quality of drama
s on The Great

Bard's himself

b) How quickly de

limited our
continuing

choice for lin
guistic express

iveness individ

c) ual character-

depth and a to
tally comprehen

sive world–
view become

s.

Are high-qual

ity painting
s oft statical

ly framed
that they be

come alivened
through our

own creative-
receptiv

ity.

Card player (2)

a) s wasting their

time away if

only exposed to
that tension

ed–touch of
I've done it

b) right while

the cards keep

escaping to
their own self–

desiring route.

Eye to eye

the magnetic
length of a

shortening
self-expos

ure.

Our little *(3)*

a) so very active

harmless ap

pearing amia
ble "security

b) man" secured

little here

except a post-
retirement

job and an in

c) disputable

hard-of-hear
ing repetitive

initiating
style.

Those who (2)

a) question poetry

as only an

ornamental
embellishment

of every day
life should

b) realize that

what seems so

"ordinary" may
depth more than

what they're
actually exper

iencing.

Patriotic (8)

a) historical

writing may

assure one's
readers (and

b) oneself) of

one's genuine

national sym
pathy but

may also impli

c) citly disregard

even the attempt
of an at least

many–sided
historical–

d) objectivity

Why did America

need an aristo
cratic foreign

(French) obser

e) vor (de Tocque

ville) almost
two centurie

s ago to real
ize the problem

f) atic achieve

ments of our

fledgling demo
cracy and another

g) French theorist

Montesquieu

to source the
essential

checks-and-balan

h) ces of what

democracy most-
need

s.

These long-

　　　leafed palm
　　　s convey a

　　　processional
　　　sense of adorat

　　　ion their bran
　　　ches extending

　　　in praise of
　　　their distant

　　　but invisibly
　　　creative–master.

For Warren (2)

　　　a) Those depthed

　　　to a self-en

　　　closing bibli
　　　cal faith how

　　　ever certain

　　　b) may not be pre

　　　pared for The
　　　Lord's myster

　　　iously creat
　　　ive otherwise

　　　ness.

Those too (4)

   a) careful of a

life-time mate

framed their
one-and-only

   b) into a port

rait of their

own pre-conciev
ed expectation

s She missed
the boat or

   c) she may have

boarded the

wrong one
brilliantly

flagged but

d) sailing a route

of its own
self-accord

s at opposite
ends from her

own.

"*And they (4)*

a) lived happily

ever after"

as if love a
lone guarantee

s a future

b) happiness

but even love
can fail if

not timely re
newed if taken-

c) for-granted

if other prior

ities inter
cede Marriage

s (or at least
some) may have

d) been "made-in-

heaven" but

we're here
still very-much

earth-bound.

She was the

type who from
the very-be

ginning play
ed-all-her-

cards-out
without allow

ing for a
fully-ripen

ed-recept
ive-response.

With the *(2)*

a) tides going-out

he felt much

of the same
horizoned

to the dis

b) tancing where

abouts of spac
iously forgott

en-remembr
ance

s.

Still having *(4)*

a) trouble to per

spective her

just-right
motherly-felt

with the mi

b) grant's (having

no children
of her own)

and their
learning a for

eign language

c) without having

mastered their
own She self–

sufficient
in her appear

ance yet some

d) how needed a

why and where
fore in her

aging year
s.

We all know *(2)*

a) that look of

naughty child

ren misbehav
ed spouse

s and traffic
offender

b) s Better not

to police them

looking aside ap
pearing despite-

all innocent
ly self-content.

Walking-the- *(3)*

a) beach may prove

for some as

but a daily
routine for o

b) thers a thought

ful interlude

and yet for
even still o

thers a listen
ing for one'

c) s own step

s listening–

back dialogu
ing self-suffi

cience
s.

Flag-pledging (2)

a) allegiance

s remains

strangely for
eign for my

double identi
ty–claim

b) s to Christ

my saviour and

to the Jewish
people so often

purposed-in-
blood.

The gulls

levelling
their sound

less distanc
ings until

the sands
flattened-

down in night-
timed obscur

ity.

Benn's poem

s so heavily
charged with

profusive i
magery modern

or not his
poems lack that

most necessary
breathing space

fulness.

As Ely Cathe *(3)*

a) dral seems ri

sen-from-the-

sea untouch
ably Christian

b) yet somehow

primevally

awakened from
its own pre-

origined past
Benn's verse

senses much-of-

c) the-same though

scarcely origin

ed from a tru
ly Christian

ed calling.

Benn's earl *(3)*

a) iest poems so

inhaling the

dead's dying
aroma left

b) his verse (and

person) so dis

tanced from any
thing approach

ing beauty

c) more a person

al closeness
to the ugliest

of life's time-
telling truth

s.

This daily

changeability
of clouds as

a heavenly re
hearsed artist

ic performance
of continual

ly unlimited
poetic stream–

lined appearan
ces.

That continual (5)

a) divide in Ameri

can politics

as proof of
both political

parties' prefer

b) ence for their

own party's-sake
than for the

country's well–
being also con

c) vinces other

nations to hold

to their own
authoritarian

one-man rule

d) 's easier for

decision-making
We American

s are on world-
display and

e) "America first"

may help first o

ther nation
s as well.

Our time-shar (5)

a) ing move down-
the-hall from
347 to 343 room
ed–in almost i

b) dentical enclos
ures that only
the numerical
change answer
s our daily

c) questioning
whereabout
s somehow re
minding of
those numbered

d) nameless Jew

s waiting that

long-deciding
line for immed

iate death or a

e) last almost i

dental death-
deciding number-

game.

They even *(2)*

a) swim or stand

in the water

here beer-hold
ing secure

ly sourced
to the simultan

b) *eous taste of*

that popular

beverage'
s appeal and

the Floridian
water's uplift

ing know-how.

Reflection

s in water re
affirming

these wind-
swept discord

ant images of
what kept him

so uneasily
soul-search

ing.

Some of (2)

a) *these highly*

weighted mid-

western wo
men seem more

like old-fash
ioned tank

b) s discarded

when the war

no longer re
quired their

most necess
ary mobilisat

ion.

This Flori

dian sun re
spects nothing

but its own
time-holding

shadowing
s.

One doesn't *(7)*

a) know these day

s who'll be

preaching what
This guest-one

b) 's almost com

pletely lost

voice but con
veyed through

hands eyes and

c) a strange way

of sinking-down
almost to

bottom-ground
of what he

d) called "the

secret place"

didn't seem
so secret to

me but his

e) message could

have been con
densed to 3

continually
repeated sen

f) tences Secret

or not I hoped

for a rhetoric
cal short-cut

but that "se

g) cret place" e

longated as a
snake's secret

ly self-enclos
ing intent.

At the moment *(3)*

a) nothing's look

ing-back to

dialogue this
me-too poem

b) It may after-

all have be

come routin
ed my problem

creative tens
ion can't be

c) taken-for-grant

ed So it must

for a recept
ively fruitful

dialogue.

Do we read *(6)*

a) because we want

to be entertain

ed like first-
rowed for a

b) movie that's

really a most

personal dream-
sequence Really

good prose should

c) reveal a depth

ed–character-
study often as

with Jane Austen
or Henry James

d) a pertinent

and linguisti

cally appropriate
dialogue or it

may as with

e) Thomas Hardy and

Herman Melville

also be charact
erized through a

mysterious re
lation between

f) person and

place why then

a lasting need
for poetry?

Is it really *(6)*

a) possible to be

come bored with

one's own per
son (I've

b) known several

when it become

s even-more
than possible)

For some their

c) life's been

so routined
that there seem

s no-possible-
way-out Best

d) then to exchange

it for another

self (we all
possess many un

discovered one

e) s) the one

(for example) we'
ve left behind

or always want
ed to become

Life's waiting

f) to be dialogued

You yourself
must chose to

be lined–up
first and only.

Kisses when

warmly-felt and
deeply-desired

open-up that
secret door

to the whole
ness of a

thoroughly
bodied-fulfill

ment.

It's become (2)

a) Florida again

no longer dis

guised in a
cooled winter

stay-at-home
And the sun'

b) s resolved to

perpetuate

its really
down-south warm

ful expectat
ions.

Somewhere

sometime (but
rarely) Benn'

s poetry unif
ies a say-so

of thought-
felt self-deny

ing imagery –
A poet is

(however seld
om) new-born.

Benn's music

persistently
sings of an

always other
wise It become

s of one's
own blood if

self-deceiv
ing.

One want *(6)*

a) s to say to

Octavio Paz

slow-down
collect your

b) thoughts let

them speak in

silent rever
ence to their

sustained mean

c) ing Let them

newly reveal
the most necess

ary time–
lengths Paz'

d) poetry of ex

cessive off–to–

the–races (Hope
you haven't

forgotten

e) your ticket)

listening
back as if

time could be
come appropriat

f) ed to the

now as alway

s foreword
ing.

That palm

tree has a
lot to tell

us at night
lit to a grace

ful darkly in
habiting ex

pressive
ness.

Floridian (2)

> *a) nights myster*
>
> iously alive
>
> to the palm'
> s through–
>
> flowing awaken

> *b) ings as these*
>
> tidal wave
> s transform
>
> ing their out–
> reaching dark
>
> nesses.

These primev (2)

> *a) al Floridian*
>
> darknesses
>
> depthed a time
> when Indians
>
> inhabited
> these land

b) s and the

moon still wit

nessing the
spirit's satis

fying sacrifi
cial-offering

s.

Florida *(2)*

a) once swamp-

lands inhabit

ed by cere
moniously

colored snake
s and the

b) Indian's se

cret awareness

of their invis
ible untouch

ably poison
ous claim

s.

She learned *(3)*

a) to paint accord

ing to those

tradition
al rules of

color perspect

b) ive and accent

uating purpose
s whereas I

quite independ
ently sensed

my quite inde

c) pendently

most personal
ly involving

word–sense.

Childless (3)

a) yet gifted with

a protective

maternal in
stinct wombed

in the need

b) s and care

s of their
half-timed

dog who died
when the other

half-time of

c) his most scent

ed purposing
s pre–determin

ed his distant
and untimely

death.

In memory Octa (2)

a) *vio Paz The de*

sire may be

round fruit
fully-sourced

temptingly-
near my hand

b) *s holding for*

their home-

based thought
s as these

winds time-en
compassing.

So-called

"major poem
s growthed of

minor seed
's necess

ary time-re
calling word-

insistencie
s.

What I once *(2)*

a) knew erased

in a time–in

tending forget
fulness I

wanted it
back called a

b) live but it

failed to

hear Now I
sense time'

s once–told
vacancy.

Florida' *(5)*

a) s become very-

much Ponce de

León's fount
aining garden

b) of youthful

thoughts but

its flat dull
ed plained mid–

western dia

c) lect seems in

appropriate
ly prosaic and

its card–game
s and cheap

d) novels unatten

tive to the

real beautie
s that should

encompass

e) their primar

ily inspiring
youthful memor

ies.

Reading Paz *(4)*

a) and Benn alter

nately writing

my own that
their rhythmic

b) insistencie

s may have

been reestablish
ing my own Or

perhaps more

c) like Ives' poly

tonal two pat
riotic 4th of

July bands
meeting discord

d) antly at the

center of Dan

bury Connecti
cut.

Softly sub *(2)*

a) dued cloud

s cushioned

in a Florid
ian timely re

sponse that e
ven such re

b) current pain

s seem as if

soothed in
to a respons

ive familiar
ity.

Often too (2)

a) close to life

the poem step

s back perspect
ing time's un

evening flow
listening

b) shadows and

the self-per

petuating now
as if unreal

ly there be
fore.

These peli (3)

a) cans haven't

changed their

pre–aspiring
course surfac

ing the wave

b) s gliding the

sky's sound
lessly apparent

realms We mean
nothing to

their daily

c) poetic flight

s envision
ing more of

what we've
mainly left be

hind.

The poem (2)

a) certains its

own selective

ways taking
this leaving

that because
each word–i

b) mage cause

s a meaning of

its own not
really our

s yet private
ly sanction

ed.

I'm not look (2)

a) ing for self-en

dangered place

s but for
those seclud

ed ones some
where in the

b) pre-discover

ed backwater

s of what
was once quiet

ly fabled in un
answering solit

udes.

If you've (2)

a) found your voice

It's like that

instrument
you've played

for year
s now resound

b) ing in the

blood–pulsing

of your very-
being no-wheres-

else but now.

These wave

s receding in
to the remem

brances of
what seemed

lost but now
renewing

those redis
covered dream

ed-reverie
s.

Is faith a (4)

a) pre-condition

for fully under

standing Christ
ian culture

b) or can an in

depthed train

ed humanist
read himself

into what
still remain

c) s foreign to

his raison d'ê
tre One used

to think an
Asian couldn'

d) t interprete

the different

iated Viennese
classics We

were wrong.

Man's emanci *(13)*

a) pation from God

now completely

guaranteed
There's no

b) need for a Creat

or History'

s a seculariz
ed discipline

and we can de

c) termine our

own sex and
even the way

s and mean
s of our life'

d) s end We're

completely e

mancipated to
an all-command

ing unspeak

e) able loneliness

and a life
that's lost

its sense-for-
meaning When

f) it's no long

er fashionable

to be a devout
Christian

g) That once fash

ionable Christ
ian heritage

has been re
placed by a

h) truly existen

cial need for

a self-emanci
pation Can we

retrieve a once

i) pre-determin

ing Christian
culture when

believers them
selves remain

j) more fixed on

self-salvation

and when that
once Christian

culture's lost

k) its most essential

origins Man's

not enough
he's become per

l) petually en

slaved in de

humanizing
ideologie

s and by his
own thirst for

m) a Baal god that

satisfies his

flesh but not
his uncertain

ed spirit.

Are these (2)

    a) waves "but the

    meaningless

    plungings of"
    light and sound

    or are they
    constant remind

    b) ers that time

    will always re

    main with us
    despite wars sick

    nesses and e
    ven famine.

Some artists (3)

    a) of all kind

    s may judge

    others while
    revealing

    more of their

b) own self-satis

fying aesthet
ics Others may

look for qualit
ies denied

themselve

c) s still other

s as myself may
judge this

way or even
that way as

well.

Steven Foster (2)

a) America's minor

Schubert home

s one to a
familiarity

of many place
s where he'

b) d either never

lived or homed

for a short
time song–senti

mentally–length
ening.

Have these (2)

a) waves washed-a

way my sand–

reaching
thoughts left

helplessly

b) sea-bound

until bottom
ed to a resi

due of frag
mented design

s.

"A man and

a woman are
one" however

we've been
separate

ly joined
exclusively

timed to a
unified whole

ness substan
tially samed.

Maids work

ed for one
world yet liv

ed in another
Their allegian

ce only certain
ed by the child

ren they har
boured from a

self-demand
ing society.

Either right (4)

a) or wrong but

in this case

neither one
nor the other

b) It's somewhere

inbetween

as that no–
man's–land bet

ween two oppos

c) ing armies

or waiting for
a final resolut

ion (if there
is any) of what

d) remains neither

here nor (e

ven tentative
ly otherwise)

there.

The army a

place to learn-
a-trade and

to learn to
kill an in

stinct awaken
ed in our most

primeval
ly-sourced

blood-length
s.

When word (2)

a) s thought

s and mood-

tonalitie
s fail to re

spond to a
unifying whole

b) leaves the

poet perpetual

ly side-lined
for a time-in

voking chance
appearance.

The four-of- (3)

a) us more or less

in our 80s

reflecting
the fortunate

b) self-reveal

ing ways life

seems to have
been pathed for

us pre-determin
ing or simply

c) the luck of

the right time

and place so
personally re

sponding.

Yearly Ft.

Myers' friend
s perennial

ly flowering
of what has be

come so pre-es
tablishing

rightly-sourc
ed.

I knew from

the very beginn
ing I'd become

empty-hand
ed because of

those reserved
seats So I

took to the
back-rows

waiting for
those reserved

to begin empty
ing-out.

In a good (4)

a) marriage it

seems from

what I hear
and daily ex

b) perience Wo

men mainly de

cide but with
the border–

line mostly

c) not so clear

ly defined
Even today

wives most
often establish

d) the home-bred

stability of

a two–sided
marriage.

Then at that (3)

a) fatal age of 18

just as far a

way as possible
(even in the

b) clothed-clos

et) from my

parent's self-
securing me as

hooked–fish

c) imprisoned

in the help
lessness of

a no–ways–
out.

If these (3)

a) self-declar

ed words con

tinue to boy
cott me I'll

just have to
think-them–

b) *in to my pre*

establish

ed mosaic of
idea poem

s standing

c) *on their own*

4 footed in
stinctive

ly effective
know–how.

If most of (2)

a) *the great Ameri*

can tycoons

with less than
a highschool

diploma It's
not surprising

b) *this anti-cult*

ural emphasis

at the monied
heart of Ameri

ca's business–
thinking

s.

Off-white

sands secur
ing my mind'

s length to
a distancing

of unfamiliar
speechless

ly evoking wave-
sense origin

s.

Poems must (4)

a) *begin themselve*

s out of the

obscuring
darkness

b) es discerning

what remains un

said until their
reticent voice-

awakening

c) s if only for

the few but
then especial

ly cherished
as the oyster

d) ed pearl open

ed to its

hidden secret
expressive

ness.

Go right a *(3)*

a) head The Good

Lord invoked us

to voice the
names of the

b) animals individ

ually conceived

one by one as
He had voiced

us to that

c) particular life

named for Now
and alway

s self-invok
ing then.

Manatees (4)

a) shadowing

those water

s with the
scarcely visi

b) ble outline

s of their

peaceably o
ver-weighted

shyness If

c) Columbus envis

ioned them as
mermaids either

his eye-sight
or more so

d) his aesthet

ic sensibil

ity must have
constantly

failed him.

These thorough *(2)*

a) ly entangled

Floridian tree

s leave my
mind-sense dir

ectioned in

b) so many way

s as those poeti
cally time-re

claiming re
source

s.

Words that

don't sound
the way they

mean are mis
placed misnam

ed outside
the bound

s of what'
s poetical

ly appropri
ate.

Is it poss (2)

a) ible to be

neutrum sex

ually lack
ing an in

stinct for

b) what purpose

s us to re
lease those

most intimate
ly aroused

tension
s.

Preaching a (3)

  a) one-way street

  paved through

  the heart of
  each and e

  b) very's self-

  defining rai

  son-d'être
  Whereas the

  poem's at the

  c) crossways of

  its own two–
  wayed time-pre

  cluding identi
  ty–cause.

For Leroy

Rarely has a
nother stood

at my vacant
place voicing

the other-side-
of self's in

tricately ex
posing pre

sence.

Cats may (3)

a) best understand

the unravelling

intricacie
s of why the

b) poem's become

as a ball-

of-wool time-
recalling its

own cat and

c) mouse here and

there of an o
therwise reveal

ing game-
sake.

If the poem (3)

a) demands its own

right-of-say

while I'm wait
ing for it's

b) often unexpect

ed appearance

It' because
that poem's

its own master
(or so it

c) *thinks) and*

I'm but a ser

vant to its
form–demanding

identity–cause.

Those as (3)

a) *Leroy and Tom*

with numerous

and varied aca
demic degree

b) *s realize more*

of The Good

Lord's creat
ive innovating

a mysterious
labyrinth of

c) *what they've*

come to rea

lize as their
own iden

tity-cause.

If as I was (4)

a) *told "your poe*

try's better

than you" I'
d prefer it

b) *speaking on*

its own term

s until I dis
covered that

we'd become

c) two-sides of

the same David
Jaffin though

the poem con
tinues to be

d) come the more

of my own

identity–
cause.

I never be (4)

a) lieved in the

possibility

of lyrical
cows until

b) Franz Marc

tried to con

vince me o
therwise I

wouldn't e

c) ver try to

milk poems out
of their essent

ial there-be
ing off to

d) Marc's (and

their) twice

weekly dance-
rehearsal

s.

What Matthew *(3)*

a) Arnold heard

and Sophocles

centuries be
fore him I

listened

b) as hard as I

positively
could but heard

nothing of
that voiced to

its unknown

c) source time

and tide's con

tinuously
rhythmic en

velopping
s.

Waiting for (2)

a) *what will most-*

likely not happ

en's like those
untimely pause

s at the com
ings and go

b) *ings of the*

train-station

feeling an un
easing sense

of just sitt
ing-still.

A cloud-dis

playing process
ional spaceous

ly transform
ing the blue–

skied impress
ionably unknown

receptivity.

Most long (3)

a) poems outdo them

selves should

have left–off
long before

b) as many such

sermons But those

chosen remnant
s when the word

s needed litt
le–more than

c) their own self-

purposing committ

ments These will
remain time-and-a

gain.

Shadow

s of palm
s over-tell

ing that un
certained

length of lyri
cally convey

ing transpar
encie

s.

When they've

the right list
eners the poem

sanctifie
s its own

cause awaken
ing to a

time-intend
ing constan

cy.

The poems of (2)

a) Gottfried Benn

not a

word however
veiled of

Hitler of the
Jew's plight

b) just a self-

dialogue of

words darkly
unrevealing

his pre-assum
ing self.

Chopin (3)

a) What need does

a piano-compos

er have for
grand operas

and symphonie

b) s or even the

intimacies
of chamber

music when
his finger

s repeatedly

c) defining the

time-length
of his self–

recording
sensibiliti

ies.

Benn's self- *(3)*

a) sufficiency

at the death–

knell of Ger
man culture

b) mirror an un

believable

arrogance
quite equival

ent to those

c) severely

blood–lett
ing pagan

time
s.

If animal (2)

a) s instinctive

ly realize

well–in–advance
of natural catas

trophic time–
tellings Should

b) n't we be quest

ioning the suppos

ed superior
ity of our most

advanced scienti
fic–meth

ods.

For Carol and Warren *(4)*

a) It almost em

barassed me
being seated at

b) the head of

the table at
a small gather

ing of most
illustrious

c) persons King

David of old

a poet reigning
only through the

quality of his

d) aging knight

s and still
attractive

ladie
s.

An early

morning invasion
of black bird

s tree-bound
darkening the

heaven's shadowed-
foreboding

s.

Florida today' (5)

a) s like a two-
sided self the
tourists retir
ed Northerner

b) s their golf
courses seafood
restaurant
s but little
has changed

c) those poetical
ly accumulat
ing sandied beach
es the lyrical
and ever stabil

d) izing palm tree

s and that

self-display of
exotic birds

the leaping
mullets and most

e) especially

those once In

dian-snaked still
deviously myster

ious back-water
s.

A *true Southern*

er's real South'
s inland where

there's a contin
uity of time

and place black
and white

still separate
most certain

ly not equal
as it's always

s been and most
likely will long

remain the same
pre-establish

ing identity-
cause.

For George

Science and

faith two level
s of understand

ing parallel
means separate

ly secluded
to their own

self-retriev
ing routes but

perhaps
without real

izing why or where
unified in a

two-sided human
quest for the

same self-es
tablishing i

dentity-cause.

The best land

scape painter
s as Constable

have been land
scaped themselve

s what's seen
become dialog

ued into a
pre-establish

ing mood a
wareness.

Still life (3)

a) s have become

a most necess

ary antidote
to a restless

b) always moving-

on society

They slow-down
as the great

classical mast

c) *er's adagio*

s in self-re
flecting si

lence
s.

Historical *(2)*

a) *painters in a*

non-historical

ly oriented
society when the

past's envision
ed not on its

b) *own terms but*

on its present-

day's here-and-
now as if it

will always
s remain so.

Abstract

art can only
become abstract

ed when it's
as Charles Seli

ger so concen
trated to the

eye's length
of a coloring–

intense there-
being.

If you boy (3)

a) cott your own e

lected president

you're not
only a bad lo

b) ser but quest

ioning the de

mocratic pro
cess right–down

to its alway
s fragilely

c) rooted time-

holdings haven'

t yet reach
ed their time-

preluding end-
sake.

Waiting un (2)

a) easily for Jesus'

most necessary

2nd Coming
forgetting

that His tim
ing's entirely o

b) therwise than

your own wishful

thinking as
"a thief in the

night" He'll
come.

He didn't (2)

a) really know

what he was

looking-for
but found it

nevertheless
Dialogue'

b) s always a

two-way street
but its found

ation's already
been laid time-

deep.

You could

call it "memor
y's lane" sweetly

voiced pre-rock
and-roll from

his pre-classi
cal youth The

Bonita Spring
s antique shop

uniquely stock
ed with memor

ies that fail
ed to move him

back into
their softly

sentimental-
past.

Time-sequen (2)

a) ces may have

pre-determin

ed his life'
s expectancie'

s self-will

b) ed but never

the less new–
born from a

still irre
trievable–

past.

They may have (2)

a) taken-him-for-

a–ride but it

went smooth
ly to an un

known destinat

b) ion and once

there he felt
as if new–

born from an
irretriev

able past.

Are ancient (4)

a) ruins simply

"a remembran

ce of thing
s past" and/

b) or a continu

ity of our

most necessary
cultural and

religious

c) raison d'être

and if destroy
ed have they

also signalled
the futility

d) of man's becom

ing reconciled

to his self–
destructive

instinct
s.

If some shell (6)

a) s still re

tain the voice

of the sea
Are they still

b) listening to

what's irrevo

cably past
or is the voice

they hear

c) the ever-pre

sent echoing
of what remain

s inextinguish
ably so Have we

d) too become hori

zoned beyond

our own length
for realizing

why time's con

e) tinually justi

fying itself
even when our

times have be
come envision

f) ed beyond their

no-wheres time–

envelopp
ing.

This poem *(2)*

a) started-off

without dis

cerning its
true intent

which I as

b) well failed

to discover
its most gen

uine need for
realizing–

why.

Do those

> walking-the-
> beach at this
>
> early hour
> still more
>
> than less–in
> volved in that
>
> nightly dream-
> sequence until
>
> the repeating
> sounds of the
>
> waves washed it
> back to its
>
> origined
> necessity.

We've been (6)

> *a) warned not to*
>
> judge other
>
> s or we'll
> be judged by
>
> *b) The Good Lord*
>
> through the
>
> same measure
> of our own
>
> self-certain

c) ty But what

of the elect
ed judge who

must daily
judge accord

d) ing to the

measure of man–

made laws im
perfectly

sourced Should
the law contin

e) ually mirror

the spirit of

changeable
times or should

an imperfect
constitution

f) become the e

ternal mea

sure of man'
s own sense–

of-justice.

"*Thou shall* (6)

a) love thy

neighbor as

thy self" the
"golden rule"

b) so tarnished

by self-in

terest I well
know who ans

wered "I'm in

c) capable of

loving myself
How then can

my own unlov
ing self be

required to

d) love other

s" Such an
evasive ans

wer reminds me
of my cousin

David who said

e) "I believe

and live by
all of the 10

commandment
s except that

very-first one

f) which I told

him was the
ground-base

measuring–rod
of all-the-

other
s.

The major (3)

a) essential life-

themes as

birth love
aging death

remain the

b) lasting source

of poetic re
levance If ne

glected such
secondary

poetry lack

c) ing in timeless

ly enduring
meaning will

soon become en
tirely forgott

en.

"It's not

easy poetry" de
manding a con

centrated ef
fort to resolve

its oft in
tricate time–

tellings – Was
good poetry e

ver easily self–
certained.

Is the sea (2)

a) personally voic

ed wherever

shored for its
time–coming mess

age Or are
these waves as

b) any others im

personally

sanctioned
for their al

ways–samed in
voking–reach.

Still life

s oft acti
vate our dor

mant sense
s Or they

may abstract
what's insuffi

ciently self–
involving.

Surprise (4)

a) s of most any

kind awaken

unexpected
yet deeply

b) elevated

coloring

s They catch
us unbalanc

ing our daily

c) steadfast

ness demanding
an otherwise

appeal on
their own term

d) s they replen

ish what may

have seemed
less then self–

enduring.

This sea'

s too vast
to enclose my

pre-forming
need for an

encompass
ing and yet

completely
satisfying

wholeness.

High-tide (2)

a) the waves sound

as Beethovenian

expressive-
fullness over

flowing what

b) ever resistance

would stand-
up to its

most conclusive
clashing-sonor

itie
s.

A young mo

ther baby-in-
arms dialogu

ing its speech
less though

neverthe
less respons

ive heart-
pulsing
s.

It-may-have- (2)

a) *been familiar*

ground once

seen and known
but now after

years of va
cancy it take

b) *s-on its pri*

mary appear

ance untouch
ably primev

al virgin–land
once–again.

Most good (2)

a) poems have

learned to en

dure their
own sense-of

mystery Why
then try to ex

b) plain what

doesn't want

to be known
at least in

that most-limit
ed-way.

Pelican

s surfacing
the winds with ·

out thought
s or care

s of anything
other than

their express
ively time-drift

ing solitude
s.

A distant

city raised
from stone-i

magining a
wareness to

a fathomed
height of un

touchably-
secured self–

certainty.

Sanderling

s scattering
their feet-im

pressioned
left behind

touch–or–find
abandoned–

surfacing
s.

If only Paz

had learned
the Webern-

way of cutt
ing-down to

an irreducib
ly refining

jewelled-pre
sence.

Have these

beaches elongat
ed my hesitant

steps even
beyond their

soundless im
pression

s indelibly
pre-determin

ed.

The Dutch *(2)*

    a) built dykes pro

tecting them

from the wa
ter's overflow

ings and she
found protect

    b) ive means as

well to keep

reliably in
tact her so

often overflow
ing too-much-

of-self.

The more names *(2)*

    a) have become in

itialled es

pecially
for in-group

disciple
s the less

b) such a mini-

language re

veals its
truly need

ed intention
s.

The mute (2)

a) silences of

these sandy

beaches extend
ing my own

sensitized
off-white a

b) wakening

s into the

loneliness
of time's for

saken distan
cing

s.

When desert

flowers become
sourced-in–

stone they
blossom a

seldom reward
ing colored–

expressive
ness.

Inspiration *(6)*

a) 's a romantic

concept for an

almost magic
ally self-re

b) leasing poet

izing yet I pre

fer "dialoguing"
because those na

kedly-exposed

c) words must first

reclaim their
self-reflect

ing soul–sense
before the poet

d) can craft that

inevitable

calling into
its pre-ordain

ed meaning

e) s It's not the

Holy Spirit
whispering

those pre-giv
en divinely inspir

ed words but an

f) unidentifi

able spirit
nevertheless

attaining the
height of its

own self-fulfill
ment.

A perfect (3)

a) fit when a wo

man experience

s a dress-fit
in length fab

b) ric illuminat

ing coloring

s its bodied–
closeness She

realize

c) s what a poem

would also
like to feel

no more than
that or e

ven less-so.

Those ever- (2)

a) so-repetitive

winds insisting

as the close
ly-defining-

waves their
self-express

b) iveness lang

uaged in a

pre-ordained
articulat

ing enigmat
ic time-call

ing.

These sand *(4)*

a) s have been

levelled–down

as Miss Black
burn's 2nd grade

b) blackboard

chalked–away

to its primeval
choice of clean

sed apparen

c) cies as these

sands morning–
still waiting

to be writt
en–through

d) his first

thought–attend

ing footstep

s.

Out at sea

a seldom boat
here–or–there

reclaiming
those distan

ces my eye
s have time–

sensed to
their own im

provising
poetic–hold.

High tide *(5)*

a) s as Beethoven

in c minor

overwhelming
whatever re

b) sistance he'd

learned from

Haydn and Mo
zart's classi

cal mode to

c) ensure safe

ly wrought
most satisfy

ing self-enclos
ings Haydn need

c) ed neither

triumphal

victory-claim
s nor a Schiller-

based freedom-

d) call despite

the poetic

tensions of his
storm–and–stress

time–consumat

e) ing God remain

ed steadfast

ly reassuring
his own home-

based arrival.

Missouri *(4)*

a) neither North

nor South East

nor West–mid
America it's

b) two most famous

literary son

s Mark Twain
and T. S. Eliot

marking the

c) great divide

beween the
America of Euro

pean cultural
tradition and

d) that of its

indigenous

no–wheres–else
but its own.

If one can (4)

a) become a so-

called Christian

without believ
ing in The Lord'

b) s incarnation in

Jesus' crucifix

ion of sin-
forgiveness

and the resurr

c) ection of His

Godly-sharing
of our own

future then
one can become

d) a so-called

poet without

realizing the
distinctive

word–quality of
that calling.

*In Nomine
Domini Febr.
2018*

Poetry books by David Jaffin

1. **Conformed to Stone,** Abelard-Schuman, New York 1968, London 1970.

2. **Emptied Spaces,** with an illustration by Jacques Lipschitz, Abelard-Schuman, London 1972.

3. **In the Glass of Winter,** Abelard-Schuman, London 1975, with an illustration by Mordechai Ardon.

4. **As One,** The Elizabeth Press, New Rochelle, N. Y. 1975.

5. **The Half of a Circle,** The Elizabeth Press, New Rochelle, N. Y. 1977.

6. **Space of,** The Elizabeth Press, New Rochelle, N. Y. 1978.

7. **Preceptions,** The Elizabeth Press, New Rochelle, N. Y. 1979.

8. **For the Finger's Want of Sound,** Shearsman Plymouth, England 1982.

9. **The Density for Color,** Shearsman Plymouth, England 1982.

10. **Selected Poems** with an illustration by Mordechai Ardon, English/Hebrew, Massada Publishers, Givatyim, Israel 1982.

11. **The Telling of Time,** Shearsman Books, Kentisbeare, England 2000 and Johannis, Lahr, Germany.

12. **That Sense for Meaning,** Shearsman Books, Kentisbeare, England 2001 and Johannis, Lahr, Germany.

13. **Into the timeless Deep,** Shearsman Books, Kentisbeare, England 2003 and Johannis, Lahr, Germany.

14. **A Birth in Seeing,** Shearsman Books, Exeter, England 2003 and Johannis, Lahr, Germany.

15. **Through Lost Silences,** Shearsman Books, Exeter, England 2003 and Johannis, Lahr, Germany.

16. **A voiced Awakening,** Shearsman Books, Exter, England 2004 and Johannis, Lahr, Germany.

17. **These Time-Shifting Thoughts**, Shearsman Books, Exeter, England 2005 and Johannis, Lahr, Germany.

18. **Intimacies of Sound,** Shearsman Books, Exeter, England 2005 and Johannis, Lahr, Germany.

19. **Dream Flow** with an illustration by Charles Seliger, Shearsman Books, Exeter, England 2006 and Johannis, Lahr, Germany.

20. **Sunstreams** with an illustration by Charles Seliger, Shearsman Books, Exeter, England 2007 and Johannis, Lahr, Germany.

21. **Thought Colors,** with an illustration by Charles Seliger, Shearsman Books, Exeter, England 2008 and Johannis, Lahr, Germany.

22. **Eye-Sensing,** Ahadada, Tokyo, Japan and Toronto, Canada 2008.

23. **Wind-phrasings,** with an illustration by Charles Seliger, Shearsman Books, Exeter, England 2009 and Johannis, Lahr, Germany.

24. **Time shadows,** with an illustration by Charles Seliger, Shearsman Books, Exeter, England 2009 and Johannis, Lahr, Germany.

25. **A World mapped-out,** with an illustration by Charles Seliger, Shearsman Books, Exeter, England 2010.

26. **Light Paths,** with an illustration by Charles Seliger, Shearsman Books, Exeter, England 2011 and Edition Wortschatz, Schwarzenfeld, Germany.

27. **Always Now,** with an illustration by Charles Seliger, Shearsman Books, Bristol, England 2012 and Edition Wortschatz, Schwarzenfeld, Germany.

28. **Labyrinthed,** with an illustration by Charles Seliger, Shearsman Books, Bristol, England 2012 and Edition Wortschatz, Schwarzenfeld, Germany.

29. **The Other Side of Self,** with an illustration by Charles Seliger, Shearsman Books, Bristol, England 2012 and Edition Wortschatz, Schwarzenfeld, Germany.

30. **Light Sources,** with an illustration by Charles Seliger, Shearsman Books, Bristol, England 2013 and Edition Wortschatz, Schwarzenfeld, Germany.

31. **Landing Rights,** with an illustration by Charles Seliger, Shearsman Books, Bristol, England 2014 and Edition Wortschatz, Schwarzenfeld, Germany.

32. **Listening to Silence,** with an illustration by Charles Seliger, Shearsman Books, Bristol, England 2014 and Edition Wortschatz, Schwarzenfeld, Germany.

33. **Taking Leave,** with an illustration by Mei Fêng, Shearsman Books, Bristol, England 2014 and Edition Wortschatz, Schwarzenfeld, Germany.

34. **Jewel Sensed,** with an illustration by Paul Klee, Shearsman Books, Bristol, England 2015 and Edition Wortschatz, Schwarzenfeld, Germany.

35. **Shadowing Images**, with an illustration by Pieter de Hooch, Shearsman Books, Bristol, England 2015 and Edition Wortschatz, Schwarzenfeld.

36. **Untouched Silences**, with an illustration by Paul Seehaus, Shearsman Books, Bristol, England 2016 and Edition Wortschatz, Schwarzenfeld.

37. **Soundlesss Impressions**, with an illustration by Qi Baishi, Shearsman Books, Bristol, England 2016 and Edition Wortschatz, Schwarzenfeld.

38. **Moon Flowers**, with a photograph by Hannelore Bäumler, Shearsman Books, Bristol, England 2017 and Edition Wortschatz, Schwarzenfeld.

39. **The Healing of a Broken World**, with a photograph by Hannelore Bäumler, Shearsman Books, Bristol, England 2018 and Edition Wortschatz, Cuxhaven.

40. **Opus 40**, with a photograph by Hannelore Bäumler, Shearsman Books, Bristol, England 2018 and Edition Wortschatz, Cuxhaven.

Book on David Jaffin's poetry: Warren Fulton, **Poemed on a beach,** Ahadada, Tokyo, Japan and Toronto, Canada 2010.